FRUIT OF THE SPIRIT

I Want to Know

About the

Rick Osborne and K. Christie Bowler

Zonderkidz

The Children's Group of Zondervan Publishing House

For Lightwave
Managing Editor: Elaine Osborne
Art Director: Terry Van Roon

The Fruit of the Spirit copyright © 1999
by The Zondervan Corporation.

Artwork and Text copyright © 1999 by Lightwave Publishing Inc.
All rights reserved. http://www.lightwavepublishing.com

Scripture portions taken from the *Holy Bible, New International Reader's Version* Copyright © 1994, 1996 by International Bible Society.

Contributing Artists: Lil Crump–pp. 30, 31; Mark Herron–p. 29; Andrew Jaster–pp. 12, 13; Chris Kelesinski–pp. 5, 14; Keith Locke–p. 26; Ken Save–pp. 8, 9, 19; Kevin Miller—Poem on p. 27; Chester Goosen–Photos on pp. 16, 32.

The photos used on pages 9 and 24 were obtained from Corel Corporation's Professional Photo CD collection.
The photos used on pages 4, 14, and 22 were obtained from ISMI's Master Photos Collection, 1895 Francisco Blvd. East, San Rafael, CA 94901-5506.
The photos used on pages 17 and 29 were obtained from Wood River Gallery © 1997.

Library of Congress Cataloging-in-Publication Data

Osborne, Rick, 1961– .
    About the fruit of the Spirit / Rick Osborne and K. Christie Bowler.
        p.   cm.—(I want to know™)
        Summary: Introduces basic concepts about God, the Bible, and Christian living and demonstrates how to develop a relationship with God and practice Christian principles.
        ISBN 0–310–22096–3 (hardcover)
        1. Fruit of the Spirit—Juvenile literature.
    2. Christian children—Religious life—Juvenile literature.   [1. Christian life.]   I. Bowler, K. Christie, 1958– . II. Title. III. Title: Fruit of the Spirit.   IV. Title: I want to know about the fruit of the Spirit.   V. Series: Osborne, Rick. I want to know™.
    BV4571.2.073   1999
    248'.82—dc21
                                                  98-51513
                                                         CIP
                                                          AC

This edition is printed on acid-free paper and meets the American National Standards Institute Z39.48 standard.

Zonderkidz
The Children's Group of Zondervan Publishing House

Published by Zondervan Publishing House, Grand Rapids, Michigan 49530, U.S.A. http://www.zondervan.com

Printed in China

All rights reserved.

LIGHTWAVE
Building Christian faith in families
A Lightwave Production, P.O. Box 160 Maple Ridge, B.C. Canada V2X 7G1 http://www.lightwavepublishing.com

99 00 01 /HK/ 5 4 3 2

Contents

What Is Fruit? 4–5
  Berry Good Fruit
  Choose Your Fruit
  Paul—Freedom Fighter

The Benefits of God's Fruit 6–7
  Bad Fruit, Bad Results
  Good Fruit, Great Benefits
  Bad Things Happen to Good
      Fruit Bushes
  Galatians—Faith Only

The Growth Factor 8–9
  Slow and Steady
  Toymaker's Workshop
  Growth Happens!

Relationships 10–11
  Tasty Fruit
  Fruit Friends
  The Fruit
  Other Fruit

4

Love 12–13
    Fill 'Er Up
    Act It Out
    Practice Love

Joy 14–15
    Roller Coaster?
    Share the Joy
    Tough Time Joy

Peace 16–17
    Widget Peace
    Color You Peaceful
    Peace Proofs
    Paid For

Being Patient 18–19
    Missing: Wheels
    Wheelless Together

Being Kind 20–21
    Kind-Kid, the Superhero
    All-the-Time Hero
    Kind Truth

Being Good 22–23
    Ol' Reliable
    Listen!
    What Would Jesus Do?

Being Faithful 24–25
    They'll Be There
    God Shows the Way

Being Gentle 26–27
    President and Servant?
    Arnie Schwarzekitten
    Gentle Giant

Control Yourself 28–29
    Manager Maniac
    Choose First
    Thought Control

Still Learning 30–31

Go For It! 32
    Change Is an Adventure!

26

What Is Fruit?

Berry Good Fruit

No! This isn't a science book about apples and oranges. The Fruit of the Spirit is a different kind of fruit—it grows in lives, not plants. But there are similarities. Check this out: We're all "bushes"—but what kind? How do you know what kind of bush is growing in your backyard? You check its fruit. If you find raspberries, it's a raspberry bush. Simple. The fruit tells you what kind of bush it is because it grows according to the bush's nature. Raspberry bushes *only* produce raspberries.

The Bible, God's book, talks about how we grow fruit. Like berries, our fruit grows according to our nature. People can tell what kind of "bush" we are by looking at the fruit we grow—like how we talk or act. "Every good tree bears good fruit. But a bad tree bears bad fruit…. You can tell each tree by its fruit" (Matthew 7:17, 20).

Choose Your Fruit

A poison berry bush can't suddenly decide to grow raspberries. Its nature controls what it grows. After Adam and Eve sinned, our nature became sinful and controlled what we grew: sinful fruit like disobedience, hatred, and lying. But God loved us. He wanted a close relationship with us. He wanted us to have wonderful lives

Fruit bushes grow fruit according to their nature. What kind of fruit do you produce? Are you a tasty raspberry bush or a dangerous poison berry?

4

Jesus nailed our sinful nature to the cross when he died. Now sin doesn't control us anymore.

Paul—Freedom Fighter

In the Bible, the apostle Paul wrote about the Fruit of the Spirit, but he hadn't understood it until he became a Christian. Imagine having your whole life run by rules like how to wash, who to talk to, and how far to walk. Before Paul met Jesus, this was his life. He tried to please God by "doing the right thing" and obeying every law the Jews had. He was so sure God wanted us to just follow rules that he thought it was okay to kill Christians because they followed Jesus more than the rules.

Then Paul met Jesus. He learned that God doesn't want us to just follow rules and do right because we're supposed to. He wants to lovingly change our hearts so that we *want* to do what's right. Doing right doesn't save us—believing in Jesus and letting God change our hearts does. Suddenly Paul was free from trying to obey a bunch of rules, and God's Spirit began growing new fruit in him. Instead of *killing* Christians, Paul *became* one! He then taught that the only way to please God is to believe in Jesus and let the Holy Spirit change us. That's true freedom.

and grow beautiful fruit. So he sent his Son Jesus to help us.

Jesus lived like us but he never sinned. Then he died to pay for our sins. "When you sin, the pay you get is death. But God gives you the gift of eternal life because of what Christ Jesus our Lord has done" (Romans 6:23). When we accept what Jesus did and choose to obey God, our sinful nature loses its control over us. We get a new nature, and we're free to choose what fruit we'll grow. God comes into our lives through his Holy Spirit and helps us grow good fruit, the "Fruit of the Spirit," instead of poison berries. This fruit grows from the inside out. It starts with a loving, joyful attitude about life and spreads into all our relationships. How? Keep reading!

The Benefits of God's Fruit

Bad Fruit, Bad Results

STOP! Don't eat it! Poisonous or bad fruit can kill you! So can bad life-fruit. That's why growing good fruit is so important. The apostle Paul wrote, "The sinful nature enjoys sexual sins, impure acts and wild living. It worships statues of gods [and] evil powers. It is full of hatred and fighting, jealousy and fits of anger. It stirs up trouble, separates people into their own little groups, wants what others have, gets drunk and takes part in wild parties. People who live like that will not receive God's kingdom" (from Galatians 5:19–21).

Think what these things do to us! They lead to messed-up lives, fights, hurts, and broken hearts. They ruin relationships—with people and with God. Sin like this separates us from God. And people who grow this kind of fruit stay separated from God—forever! It's a lousy payback.

Good Fruit, Great Benefits

What about good fruit? When we let him, "the fruit the Holy Spirit produces is love, joy and peace, being patient, kind, and good, being faithful and gentle and having control of oneself" (from Galatians 5:22–23). These things build solid, awesome relationships. They make us respected and trusted and put our lives on the way to being great. Plus, we'll have a close relationship with God—forever!

God's Holy Spirit produces this fruit in us for our sake. God made the world and knows the best way to have awesome lives. And he shares the secret with us through his Spirit. He knows growing his kind of fruit will bless us. And we'll know him and be loved by him forever.

Like bushes, we can have tough times. But God makes sure we're okay. He gives us what we need to grow, just like he gives plants what they need: sunshine, water, and care.

Bad Things Happen to Good Fruit Bushes

Bugs. Tornadoes. Droughts. All these can harm fruit bushes. Just because a bush produces good fruit doesn't mean it will never be eaten by bugs, face big winds, or have trouble finding water. In the same way, letting the Holy Spirit grow his fruit in us and doing things God's way doesn't guarantee a perfect life. We'll have tough times, even times when it seems God's way doesn't work. But over the long haul it does—guaranteed! God is working our *whole* lives out. He knows exactly what he's doing. Obeying God pays.

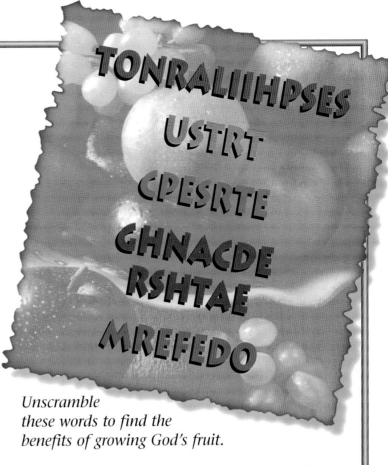

TONRALIIHPSES

USTRT

CPESRTE

GHNACDE

RSHTAE

MREFEDO

Unscramble these words to find the benefits of growing God's fruit.

Galatians—Faith Only

Paul wrote the letter of Galatians to Christians in churches he'd started. Some people had told them that believing in Jesus wasn't enough—they had to obey part of the law too. In other words, they had to follow a bunch of rules to be saved.

But Paul knew that trying to obey part of the law would trap them in the whole law—been there, done that. So he reminded them of the truth: Jesus' death paid for it all. Our works and actions don't save us—only faith in Jesus does. *All* we have to do is believe and be forgiven.

This doesn't mean we can live any way we want. No way. "Those who belong to Christ Jesus have nailed their sinful nature to his cross. They don't want what their sinful nature loves and longs for. Since we live by the Spirit, let us march in step with the Spirit" (Galatians 5:24-25). When Jesus gives us new hearts, we don't just follow rules. We follow God with our whole heart and he changes us.

The Growth Factor

Slow and Steady

How do we grow God's fruit? Slow and steady. Ever planted a seed and picked fruit from it the next day? Ever seen a newborn baby play baseball? Why not? Because life is about growth. So is the Christian life.

Once we become Christians, we aren't suddenly perfect with full-grown fruit. And God doesn't expect us to be perfect right away. Instead, we have a new beginning. "Anyone who believes in Christ is a new creation. The old is gone! The new has come" (2 Corinthians 5:17). From then on life is an adventure in growth. But we have to choose to grow. The Holy Spirit doesn't control us like our sinful nature did. We're partners with him. "My friends, continue to work out your own salvation. God is working in you" (from Philippians 2:12–13).

God knows each of us inside out. He knows what we struggle with and what we're good at. He works with us in the way that's best for us.

"Don't live any longer the way this world lives. Let your way of thinking be completely changed. Then you will be able to test what God wants for you. And you will agree that what he wants is right. His plan is good and pleasing and perfect" (Romans 12:2). Here's the process: We learn from the Bible how God wants us to behave; we pray for and accept God's help; God's Spirit helps us choose his way; and God's fruit grows.

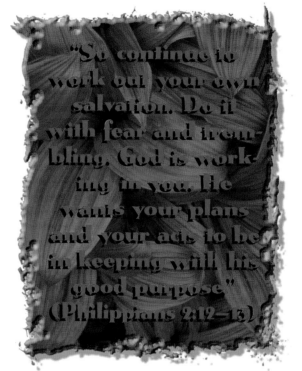

"So continue to work out your own salvation. Do it with fear and trembling. God is working in you. He wants your plans and your acts to be in keeping with his good purpose" (Philippians 2:12–13)

Toymaker's Workshop

Imagine that God is a toymaker and your life is his toy shop. Around the shop are toys at all stages of usefulness. Some are painted, polished, and perfect. Others are in the process of being carved and sanded. And others are blocks of wood that haven't even been started on.

Our lives are like that. Like those finished toys, we've learned and are ready to use some things (maybe patience). Other things are "in process," like peace, perhaps. Maybe our peace is unsteady because we struggle with worry. With God, we'll focus on peace until it's polished and ready for everyday use. Then there are things we haven't even started on, maybe self-control. Like those blocks of wood, we don't even know what it is. That's fine. When we're ready, God will bring out that block of wood and help us develop self-control.

Our lives contain things at all stages of growth and readiness. The key is not to forget what we've learned, to use it every day, and to keep learning more! "Get wisdom. Get understanding. Don't forget my words. . . . Hold on to my teaching. . . . Guard it well. It is your life" (Proverbs 4:5, 13).

Growth Happens!

Growth happens in everyday decisions. For example, say you're discussing what to do about a problem. Your friend's talking. You're impatient to say what *you* want. But down in your heart God's Spirit reminds you, "To answer before listening is foolish and shameful" (Proverbs 18:13). God wants us to be patient, so you choose to listen. You don't interrupt. You wait until he's finished.

Or say someone bumps into you in the hallway and drops her books. She yells that it's your fault. You quickly ask God for help, then choose to be kind to her. You smile and help her pick up her books.

And the fruit grows.

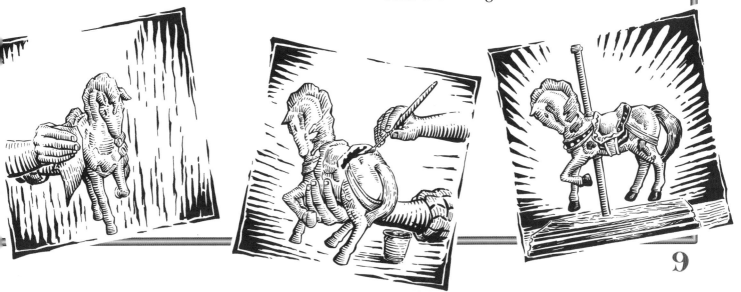

Relationships

Tasty Fruit

Now that we know how fruit grows, let's look at what it's all about: Relationships.

Sitting on your table is a bowl of juicy, freshly washed raspberries. Will you enjoy how they look, stare at them, lick your lips, then walk away? What good is fruit if you can't taste it? Pop them in your mouth and enjoy the wonderful burst of flavor. Fruit is made to be tasted.

Now, no one pops you in their mouth, but your fruit would be wasted if it wasn't tasted. Don't worry. It's being tasted by the people around you every time you act, react, or speak. How you live tells them if you're a poison berry or raspberry bush. A good test of your fruit is how you act with your family, especially your brothers and sisters. "Those who say they love God but in fact hate a brother or sister are liars. They don't love a brother or sister, whom they have seen. So they can't love God, whom they have not seen" (1 John 4:20). At home, who we really are comes out.

Fruit Friends

God's two greatest commandments are to love God and to love people (Matthew 22:37–39). They lead to the two greatest blessings: relationships with God and people. Every good relationship is based on love—the first fantastic fruit. God's fruit makes relationships work. Our friendships become stronger as our fruit grows. The more we grow God's fruit, the more we become like him. The more we become like God, the closer we grow to him and the stronger our relationships become. In fact, changing and growing in the Fruit of the Spirit is the only way to know God more and to have stronger relationships with others. What a payoff!

One for all and all for one!

Grapes never grow alone. They grow in clusters. So does the Fruit of the Spirit. We can never grow just one fruit.

others what we've received from God, and respond when things go wrong or people mistreat us.

Ready to look at each fruit? Read on. We'll show what the fruit is, what it looks like in our lives, and how to grow it. The result? A better life and loving friendships.

God's fruit helps us love and enjoy our brothers and sisters. And that makes good relationships with others a slam dunk!

The Fruit

So what exactly is this fruit? It's the nine character qualities Paul lists in Galatians 5:22–23 (page 6). He calls them "fruit," not "fruits." They all go together, like a clump of grapes. We can't decide to grow peace and ignore self-control.

To really see what the fruit is, look at God. He has them full-grown! We taste his fruit in what he's given us and how he loves and guides us. As we experience God's fruit and learn to trust him, it grows in us. We pass it on to others and God helps them grow it. It's one big cycle.

The nine fruit are in three groups. The groups have to do with how we respond to God's love, show

Other Fruit

Different places in the Bible talk about other fruit besides the nine from Galatians. Here are some of them: Being fair and doing right (Isaiah 5:7). Wisdom, understanding, respect for God, fairness, and godliness (Isaiah 11:1–5). Doing right and being true (Ephesians 5:9). Knowledge and the strength to keep going (2 Peter 1:5–7).

Jesus talked about fruit a lot, too. Check out Matthew 7:15–23; Luke 6:43–45; and John 15:1–17.

Us and God	Us and Others	Us and Tough Responses
•Love	•Being Patient	•Being Faithful
•Joy	•Being Kind	•Being Gentle
•Peace	•Being Good	•Having Control of Ourselves

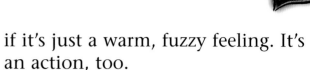

Love

Fill 'Er Up

The first three fruit are about how we respond to God. The first fruit is love. Say you live in a desert and find someone dying of thirst. You try to give him water, but your tank is bone dry. It's like trying to bake a cake with no ingredients, build a car without parts, or love when your "love tank" is empty. It can't be done.

We fill our love tank by being loved, especially by God. Like Dick is a boy, and Jane is a girl, "God is love" (1 John 4:8, 16). It's who he is—and what he does. "God loved the world so much that he gave his one and only Son" (John 3:16). And God keeps on giving. He guides, teaches, and cares for us. Love isn't love

if it's just a warm, fuzzy feeling. It's an action, too.

God's Holy Spirit produces his love-fruit in us by loving us. As we experience his love, our love tank fills up until it overflows and we have love to give away. God's love for us helps us love and forgive others. "We love because he loved us first" (1 John 4:19).

Act It Out

What is love? *An eternal commitment to give and receive unselfish thoughts, acts, and emotions.* It's a forever thing. Love doesn't drop someone because of anger or hurt. It makes relationships work. God wants us to have fulfilling, exciting relationships, so he commanded us to love. He knows love is the only way to get that. Without love, relationships die and we miss out on God's greatest blessings: loving and being loved.

So how does love work? By giving. God gave to us even when we were still deep in our sin (Ephesians 2:5; 1 John 4:9–10). Like God, we show people we love them by our actions. We listen, do little extras, hang out with them, defend and cheer them on, and give even when they don't deserve it.

But love is also a two-way blessing. Love receives. It lets others love us. It accepts their gifts, values their praise, and goes to them when we need help. It lets them love us. And get this: God not only shows his love to us, he also wants our love! He enjoys receiving it. He asks us for help with his work, wants our praise and worship, and longs for us to listen to him. Our love is precious to him, just as people's love is precious to us.

Practice Love

These tips will help you grow love. *Remember relationships are for always.* We'll be with the same people forever. Treat them lovingly now to make friends for eternity. *Recognize God in others.* Each person is special because God creates out of himself. When he made each of us, he made us out of who he is so we all reflect a part of him. Seeing God in others helps us recognize that they're wonderful, special individuals. *Respect individuality.* God made everyone different. We see, do, and think differently, and we have different likes, goals, skills, and ways of talking. Let's enjoy our differences. *Reorder your priorities.* It's natural to think of ourselves first, but love doesn't. Love puts the other person's concerns, thoughts, and desires ahead of our own.

Imagine a world where everyone loved this way!

Love is patient.
Love is kind.
It does not want what belongs to others.
It does not brag.
It is not proud.
It is not rude.
It does not look out for its own interests.
It does not easily become angry.
It does not keep track of other people's wrongs.
Love is not happy with evil.
But it is full of joy when the truth is spoken.
It always protects.
It always trusts.
It always hopes.
It never gives up.
Love never fails.
The three most important things to have are faith, hope and love.
But the greatest of them is love.
1 Corinthians 13:4–8, 13

Joy

Roller Coaster?

Remember the greatest amusement park you've ever been to? The rides, shows, and games made you happy. For how long? Until you dropped your hot dog, finished your cotton candy, or got up the next day? Happiness is like that: it comes and goes depending on what's happening. But *joy, a deep, constant, cheerful contentment,* sticks around no matter what.

When we understand that God loves us, and truly know Jesus paid for our sins, joy comes. The more we experience God's love as he's patient, kind, and good to us, the more our joy grows. Since joy grows out of who God is and his unchanging character, it's constant. Joy isn't based on circumstances, but absolutes—like knowing we have eternal life. "Always be joyful" (1 Thessalonians 5:16). "God's kingdom has nothing to do with eating or drinking. It is a matter of being right with God. It brings the peace and joy the Holy Spirit gives" (Romans 14:17).

Happiness comes from happenings. Joy comes from Jesus. Joy is the result of accepting and surrendering to God's constant love and care. He'll *never* let us down. Our joy-fruit doesn't die and drop off because something nasty happens. It's hooked into the Spirit and keeps on growing—because we know God is working everything out.

Share the Joy

Joy starts on the inside. Here are ways to grow it. *Review your "thankful" list.* Go over what God has done for you, like forgiving your sins, making a beautiful world, helping you in

Roller coasters are like happiness: lots of fun, with ups and downs, and soon over. But joy never ends because it depends on God, who is always the same.

school, giving you friends. Thank God—and watch your joy grow. *Remember how big God is*. He can handle any problem. He loves you more than you can imagine and he's looking out for you. That'll get you singing! *Rest in God's love*. Value each moment. Admire flowers, breathe fresh air, enjoy your friends. Living aware, with all your senses, increases joy. *Remind yourself of heaven*. This life is temporary. Heaven is coming up! When life gets rough, think heaven.

Like love, joy flows into our relationships as we want others to be joyful. Our gratitude attitude helps them see the positive. We encourage them, sharing stories of God's goodness and reminding them of God's love. And we share their joy. "Be joyful with those who are joyful" (Romans 12:15). But the simplest way to share joy is to turn your joy indicator on: Smile!

Tough Time Joy

God doesn't promise only good times. In fact, the Bible talks a lot about persecution and troubles. But God is always there, always in charge, and always loving. We can stay joyful even when trouble comes because we trust in God's love and care. He knows what he's doing and he'll work it all out.

"Your salvation is going to be completed. Because you know this, you have great joy. You have joy even though you may have had to suffer for a little while. Your troubles have come in order to prove that your faith is real. Though you do not see [Jesus] now, you believe in him. You are filled with a glorious joy that can't be put into words" (from 1 Peter 1:5–8). "My brothers and sisters, you will face all kinds of troubles. When you do, think of it as pure joy" (James 1:2).

Because Paul knew God, even shipwrecks couldn't take away his joy.

Peace

Widget Peace

Imagine visiting a widget factory. Suddenly a cog jams! *Ker-chunk!* Wheels *sque-e-e-al!* Belts stretch and snap. The machine *scree-ee-ches* and flings broken widgets around the factory. Look out!

That's what our lives are like without peace! We worry—about exams or what people think. We get tied up in knots and yell at friends. What a mess!

But when we have God's peace, we're relaxed and full of trust. Our lives feel like a huge, smoothly running widget machine: cogs mesh, wheels turn, belts roll, and thousands of perfect widgets are made. The more we know God's love and joy, the more confident we are that everything is working as he designed it to. Like the smooth-running factory, we're at peace. *Peace is a deep contentment and assurance that all is well because we serve a loving, wonderful*

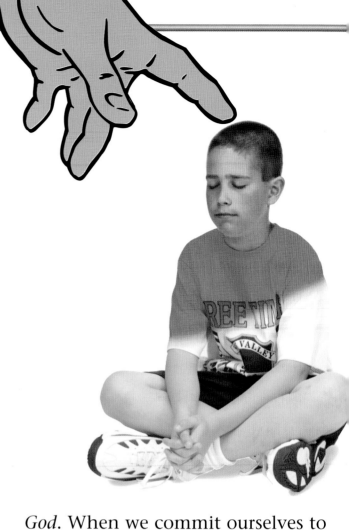

God. When we commit ourselves to God and trust him completely, he gives us perfect peace (Isaiah 26:3).

Color You Peaceful

Our peace, like love and joy, grows and spreads into our relationships. Peace inside us becomes peace between us and others. "Try your best to live in peace with everyone" (Hebrews 12:14). "Christ himself is our peace. . . . He has destroyed the hatred that was like a wall between us" (Ephesians 2:14).

Peace lets us completely relax and rest, no matter what.

Picture this: We're all black and white and God is every color imaginable. He touches us and his color flows into us. Soon we're completely colored and the color spreads into the world and people around us. That's what it's like when God, through Jesus, touches our lives with his peace. Our worries and fears calm as the color of God's peace flows in—and out to others. We paint our world with a brush of peace!

Peace Proofs

To let God's peace grow in you: *"Be still,* and know that I am God" (Psalm 46:10). Take time to be quiet and rest, thinking about God and his love. *Stay in prayer.* "Tell God about everything. Ask and pray. Give thanks to him. Then God's peace will watch over your hearts and your minds because you belong to Christ Jesus" (Philippians 4:6–7). *Stop worrying.* Jesus said, "I give my peace to you. I do not give it to you as the world does. Do not let your hearts be troubled. And do not be afraid" (John 14:27). "Don't worry about anything" (Philippians 4:6).

When the fruit of peace is growing in your life, you're satisfied and content with what you have. You have argument-free and hurt-free relationships. You're confident, knowing God is helping and guiding you. You don't fret over what might go wrong. And your friends grow peaceful, too.

Paid For

We have peace because Jesus bought it for us with his life. He made us right with God and got rid of everything that came between us. "God made peace through Christ's blood, through his death on the cross" (Colossians 1:20). "We have been made right with God because of our faith. Now we have peace with him because of our Lord Jesus Christ" (Romans 5:1). This peace doesn't depend on what's happening on the outside. Jesus' sacrifice lasts forever, so our peace is as steady as our joy. It keeps growing deeper and producing more fruit.

Jesus' death made our peace possible—peace with God and then with people.

Being Patient

Missing: Wheels

The second group of three fruit is about relating to people. As we grow in love, joy, and peace because of God's love for us, it's easier to treat others the way God treats us. For example, God's patience with us teaches us what patience is and helps us be patient with others. God's patience shows us his love.

A toymaker pushes a truck across his worktable—but it doesn't move very well. If he gets impatient and throws the truck across the shop, we'd say he has a temper. But what if the truck's wheels aren't attached yet? Then we'd say the toymaker is silly for being impatient with the truck—the truck can't help it! No toymaker would get angry at a toy for not being finished or for having missing parts.

Like that truck, we're all missing some "wheels." We're still learning how to obey, be loving, and so on. God is patient with us because he knows we're not finished. Even when Jesus was dying, he didn't get angry or impatient with those who put him there. He said, "Father, forgive them. They don't know what they are doing" (Luke 23:34). He knew they didn't understand who he was. "He put up with attacks from sinners. So think about him. Then you won't get tired" (Hebrews 12:3). The key is to remember that everyone is unfinished and growing. When someone upsets or hurts us, we need to remember that, like us, they're still learning about relationships and how to be who God wants them to be. "Be patient. Put up with one another in love" (Ephesians 4:2).

Wheelless Together

Patience is showing God's grace and patience to others, despite what they "deserve." These tips will help you develop patience: *Remember we're all in the same boat.* If it wasn't for God's work in our lives, we'd be exactly where the other person is. None of us are getting wiser, growing, and winning over sin on our own strength. It

Can you find Patient Pete among all the things going wrong in this picture? What about two happy dogs? A baby bird crossing? A movie star? Tube fun?

takes the Holy Spirit working in us. So we can pray for the Holy Spirit to work in them, too. *Recall the button.* Have you seen the buttons that say, "Please be patient, God is not finished with me yet"? Or they might just say "PBPGINFWMY." Imagine the other person wearing it—then do what it says, and treat them the way you would want to be treated. *Rewind, back up, and take a deep breath* until you can respond patiently. "A gentle answer turns anger away" (Proverbs 15:1). "Starting to argue is like making a crack in a dam. So drop the matter before a fight breaks out" (Proverbs 17:14).

The fruit of patience growing in your life will be easy to spot because you'll speak kindly, hold onto your temper, understand where people are coming from, wait without getting upset, find it easy to forgive, be relaxed when things go wrong, and find people enjoy being around you. So recognize missing "wheels" and enjoy people where they are.

Being Kind

Kind-Kid, the Superhero

As our patience grows, we'll find it easy to act it out—in kindness. God shows us his patience through his kindness. The more he's kind to us, the more we want to pass it on.

Imagine a kitten trapped in a tree. Suddenly a kid in a "Kind-Kid" costume swoops down and rescues the kitten. Kind-Kid swoops off to help someone carry groceries, then flies off to comfort a lost child.

These are acts of kindness, but is Kind-Kid truly kind? *Kindness is a loyal commitment to a relationship and to always be considerate of others' feelings in all we say and do.* Kind-Kid is performing "random acts of kindness" but not showing the fruit of kindness. He or she isn't committed to the people he or she helped. True kindness, however, is consistently, purposefully kind. It's being Kind-Kid all the time, not just swooping in for special occasions. "You are holy and dearly loved. So put on tender mercy and kindness as if they were your clothes" (Colossians 3:12). (We always wear clothes!) It's being considerate of people's feelings, being polite, going out of our way to encourage and reach out. "Be kind to everyone" (2 Timothy 2:24).

Real kindness is an all-the-time thing. In fact, a commitment to a friendship is a commitment to kindness. Imagine if every friendship understood that! Kindness never gives up on people. "[God] is kind to people who are evil and are not thankful. So have mercy, just as your Father has mercy" (Luke 6:35–36). Remember, God is committed to you. You're not growing kindness alone.

All-the-Time Hero

Here's how to develop kindness. *Think kindly.* When you're having problems with someone, imagine hearing their thoughts. They probably sound just like yours. If you want

Real superheroes are always heroes. They're committed to doing what's right and being kind all the time.

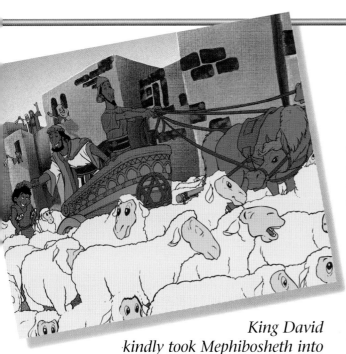

King David kindly took Mephibosheth into his own home and looked after him.

Kind Truth

Ever been asked your opinion of something ugly? Or had to tell someone their actions were wrong? God wants us to tell the truth *and* be kind, so we need to "speak the truth in love" (Ephesians 4:15). That means not blurting out, "That is so ugly it belongs in the Ugly Museum!" No way. Instead, think about the person's feelings and how you would want to be told the truth. You might say, "It's not my favorite shirt of yours. Since it has polka dots, maybe a plain shirt would look better with your checkered pants." Make sure your words help. Kindness and truth are partners working together to love people.

to defend yourself and blame the other person, guess what? So do they. If you don't want them to think badly about you, don't think badly about them. Choose to think the way you want them to.

Act kindly. Anyone can be a **Sometime** Kind-Kid. But put others first in ordinary, everyday situations, look for things to help people with, and you'll be a **Super** Kind-Kid. *Speak kindly.* Make kindness the rule for everything you say. Put a kindness filter over your mouth. "Don't let any evil talk come out of your mouths. Say only what will help to build others up and meet their needs. Then what you say will help those who listen. . . . Be kind and tender to one another" (Ephesians 4:29, 32). Have a motto, "If it's not kind, I won't say or do it!" Just watch your kindness fruit blossom!

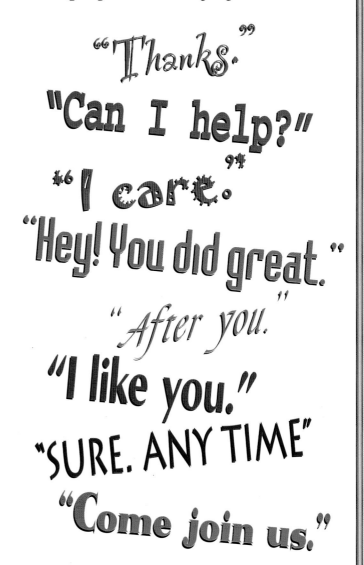

"Thanks."
"Can I help?"
"I care."
"Hey! You did great."
"After you."
"I like you."
"SURE. ANY TIME"
"Come join us."

Being Good

Ol' Reliable

VACATION, here we come! Yahoo! We're all packed and the car is loaded. But what's this? A leaking radiator? Flat tires? If the car's no good, there goes the vacation. But a *good* car will get us there every time. Why? Because when something is "good," it's reliable and consistent. A good car will get us there with no worries. We'll be relaxed, confident, and peaceful because we know we can rely on it. We can trust in goodness.

God is good—which is saying a lot: he is always reliable, perfect, honest, excellent, fair, generous, and more. "The Lord is good. When people are in trouble, they can go to him for safety. He takes good care of those who trust in him" (Nahum 1:7). God is always the same, always good and generous, always looking out for us. We can rely on him: No worries. God's consistent goodness gives us deep peace. We want to share it with others.

When God saw everything he had made, he called it very good. That's because it came out of who he is, and he is good.

For us to grow the fruit of goodness, we need to be like God. But it's not just *being* good or *not* doing *bad* things. It's *doing* good: It's choosing right over wrong. It's action. So we demonstrate what God is like to people around us. If we're good, people will know we're always there for them, always honest, always willing to do good. They'll be peaceful, knowing they can count on us.

Listen!

To grow in goodness: *Listen to your conscience.* When it tells you not to do something, don't do it! When it says, "Do good," then do it. God gave us a conscience to help us know right from wrong. The more we listen to it, the stronger it grows. "So I always try not to do anything wrong in the eyes of God and people" (Acts 24:16). But if we ignore it, our conscience weakens and our mind becomes twisted. "To people who are pure, all things are pure. But to those who have twisted minds and don't believe, nothing is pure. In fact, their minds and their sense of what is right and wrong are twisted" (Titus 1:15).

Listen to God's Spirit. Keep tuned in and sensitive to what God is saying. This means learning from the Bible what God says is right, and listening to God's Spirit in our hearts, nudging us as we go through our day. We can trust God to keep us on track.

What Would Jesus Do?

Bracelets, books, albums, Bible covers, necklaces—all with "WWJD?" Kids are wearing the jewelry, carrying the books, listening to the music, and asking, "What would Jesus do?" in various situations they face.

Just asking the question reminds us to listen to our consciences and God's Spirit as Jesus did. It reminds us, "So when we can do good to everyone, let us do it" (Galatians 6:10). "In the same way, let your light shine in front of others. Then they will see the good things you do. And they will praise your Father who is in heaven" (Matthew 5:16).

To find the answer to the question "WWJD?" check out the Bible and choose God's way. Jesus did everything God asked him to. He was completely obedient and all his actions showed God's fruit. So ask yourself WWJD? and go for God's way.

Being Faithful

They'll Be There

So God's fruit is growing in us as we live out what we learn from his love. But what happens if people respond badly? No one is perfect. Even people who love us sometimes lash out or push us away, usually because of stuff they're going through—but it hurts. That's when we really see what kind of fruit bush we are. When it's tough, will we keep being patient, kind, and good? The last three fruit are about who we really are and how we respond in tough times. The Holy Spirit uses difficult times to teach us faithfulness.

Say you had a fight with your friends last night. You promised to help them with homework today but they're late coming over. Do you wait confidently, or figure your friends changed their minds? It depends what they're like. Will they keep their commitment anyway? Are they faithful? If they are,

they'll be there. Sure enough! Here they come. They're late because one of their bikes had a leaky tire.

Faithfulness is a constant, humble commitment to God and people, and a constant expression of our loving commitment. It's always doing what we say, taking care of stuff we're responsible for, and being the same person—no matter how people act!

God Shows the Way

"He is the faithful God. He keeps his covenant for all time to come" (Deuteronomy 7:9). God is faithful even when we turn against him, sin, or don't believe him. "Will the fact that they don't have faith keep God from being faithful? Not at all! God is true, even though every human being is a liar" (Romans 3:3–4). "Even if we are not faithful, he will remain faithful. He must be true

At weddings, couples promise to be faithful to each other. From then on they trust and count on each other.

In the middle of your favorite TV show, a friend calls feeling down. You click off the TV and listen.

You drop your ice cream on the ground. You shrug and grin and get more.

You have a big test tomorrow but you're relaxed.

Your little sister drew in your favorite book. But she doesn't know any better so you don't get mad.

Your neighbor's cat knocked over the garbage in your garage—again. You willingly clean it up. When your neighbor apologizes, you smile and tell him it's okay.

You want to go with your friends but know you should go home. You choose to do right and go home.

You promised to help with your brother's science project. Even though you don't really have time, you help him.

An unpopular kid at school needs help with math. You offer to help.

You *love* junk food. But you only eat until you're full, then stop.

GENTLENESS

GOODNESS

JOY

SELF-CONTROL

PATIENCE

LOVE

PEACE

KINDNESS

FAITHFULNESS

to himself" (2 Timothy 2:13). No matter what we do, God is faithful. His love and goodness never change. He never gives up on us, stops loving us, or gets angry and says, "Serves them right!" No way. So the Holy Spirit knows about faithfulness. He can help us grow it.

When things are tough, people are mean, you want to give up, or you're tempted to do things your way, give yourself this pep talk, reminding yourself to be faithful: "God never gives up. Neither do I! God's way is the best way. God will work things out as I keep obeying. 'Let us not become tired of doing good. At the right time we will gather a crop if we don't give up'"(Galatians 6:9).

When you're growing faithfulness, your life will "taste" like this:

You can be trusted and counted on. Disagreements never end a relationship. When people get angry or hurt you, you're still patient, kind, and good to them. People relax around you because they can trust you. You're loyal, so your friendships are strong. You don't gossip, tell stories, or exclude people. You're on time and take your responsibilities seriously. You do your chores well, without complaining.

Sound too good to be true? Remember it's *God's* fruit. You don't have to be completely faithful right away. You're still learning and growing. Just keep giving yourself the pep talk and letting God's Spirit work in you. Faithfulness will grow. Guaranteed!

Being Gentle

President and Servant?

Sometimes people respond badly even when we're faithful. But then, we've done that to God and he kept right on being faithful and gentle. It's *because* God is so gentle with us and treats us so respectfully that we can be gentle with others.

Picture this: The president of the United States cleaning dirty cafeteria tables. Your principal tidying your room. Wouldn't happen? Why is it hard for even the "most important" of us to serve others? We're afraid others will think we're worth less than them. We wonder who'll look after us. Or maybe we're not sure we're valuable and loved.

But when we *are* sure, when our love tank is full and we know deep in our hearts and souls that God says we're wonderful and his children forever, it's easy to serve. As our confidence in God and in his love for us grows, we can put aside the need to be important and we can give the same constant, gentle love to others. That's what gentleness is about. *Gentleness is a quiet, inner strength that lets us serve and give to others without being threatened or feeling less than them.* It comes out of the deep confidence that God is completely taking care of our needs. We don't have to fight for respect or any of the things that stop us serving others. We can lay all that aside, knowing God has it covered—and humbly serve.

Arnie Schwarzekitten

Arnie S. is a huge man, with muscles popping out everywhere. Imagine him with a tiny kitten held gently in a hand that could bend iron. That's gentleness: Strength under control. If someone is physically gentle, they'll never physically hurt you—or a kitten. Gentleness in other areas

Gentleness treats everyone and everything carefully and tenderly.

Gentle Giant

Think of a giant as big as the sky,
with a voice ten times louder
than thunder,
legs like stone pillars,
muscles like rippling mountains,
feet that shake the earth with
mighty steps,
and eyes that flash and blaze like a
raging fire.

Then give him love twice as deep as
the ocean,
peace like falling snowflakes,
forgiveness as free as the wind,
justice that flows like rushing water,
gentleness as tender and warm as
a kitten snuggling in your lap.

This giant could destroy you.
With one thought he could consume
you with fire.
But instead he wants to be your friend,
to embrace you in mighty arms
and keep you safe from fear and harm.

Your Gentle Giant God.

---

think of yourself more highly than you should" (Romans 12:3). "Bow down to the Lord. He will lift you up" (James 4:10). Gentleness doesn't mean taking up ballet and speaking softly. It means putting others first and never hurting anyone.

So how do you grow gentleness? *Recognize you don't need to fight.* God loves you and is taking care of you. You can be gentle even when you think you should just look after yourself. *Remind yourself God loves them as much as you.* Treat them that way. *Remember the person (and their feelings) is always more important than winning—or anything else.* Let the other person be right. Being right is as meaningless as dust compared to the absolute pricelessness of the person you're dealing with. Jesus died for people, not things. *Realize the person's friendship is more valuable than anything else here on earth.* Respond only after getting things in perspective. Let gentleness grow in you. It's a beautiful fruit!

---

is just like that: it never hurts another person's feelings or dreams. It doesn't answer harshly or lash out. It's a wonderful, strong, selfless caring. Jesus said, "I am gentle and free of pride" (Matthew 11:29). We're to be like him. "Don't be proud at all. Be completely gentle" (Ephesians 4:2). A big part of gentleness is humility. "Don't

"Come to me, all of you who are tired and are carrying heavy loads. I will give you rest. Become my servants and learn from me. I am gentle and free of pride. You will find rest for your souls. Serving me is easy, and my load is light." (Matthew 11:28–30)

Control Yourself

Manager Maniac

Like love is the foundation and key to all the fruit, self-control is the foundation and key to our part in growing that fruit. We learn it from God: When he commits to do something, he always does it. He keeps his every thought, word, and action consistent with his character and commitments. He never loses control.

Jumpy Joe works at a fast-food joint but wants to be manager. He eats the food whenever he wants, comes and goes when he feels like it, and yells or throws food when he's upset. He's messy and rude. Will he ever be manager? No way. He's out of control!

Self-control is constantly deciding to do what is right, no matter how you feel. **Self**-control means we have a part in growing this fruit. We need to remember what we've already learned. Then, with self-control, we consistently choose to be a raspberry bush—not a poison berry one. The Holy Spirit helps us do what's right even when we don't feel like it. He gives us the strength not to get angry, mouth off, eat too much, steal, or be unreliable. "I will not be controlled by anything" (1 Corinthians 6:12). "People who can't control themselves are like a city whose walls are broken down" (Proverbs 25:28).

Choose First

To grow self-control: *Choose your allies.* Never forget that the Holy Spirit is working in you. "Don't live under the control of your sinful nature. . . . Live under the control of the Holy Spirit" (Romans 8:5). When

Although Jesus is God and could have called thousands of angels to help him, he controlled himself and did what God had asked him to.

you're tempted to whack your brother for doing the same annoying thing—again—that's your sinful nature. Don't choose it as your partner; ask God for help instead. *Choose right actions.* Go back over all the fruit-growing tips we've given you. God's way really is the best way to the greatest life. *Choose memory verses.* If you're having problems with something, memorize a verse about it and you'll always have it with you. (The verses in this book make good memory verses.) *Choose your words.* Always speak kindly, gently, and respectfully. "Suppose you think your beliefs are right because of how you live. But you don't control what you say. Then you are fooling yourselves. Your beliefs are not worth anything at all" (James 1:26).

With self-control you'll be confident, humble, gentle, and patient. You won't overdo anything, lie, or say nasty things. You'll work hard, turn the other cheek, help others, answer kindly, and much more. Your life will become like Jesus'. YES!

Thought Control

Just because a bird lands on your head doesn't mean you have to let it build a nest. We all have crazy thoughts. The key is not to let them make our minds their home. Chase them away! Thoughts are powerful. They're like preprogramming ourselves: What we think eventually becomes actions. So think carefully.

"Always think about what is true. Think about what is noble, right and pure. Think about what is lovely and worthy of respect. If anything is excellent or worthy of praise, think about those kinds of things" (Philippians 4:8). When a weird or bad thought comes into your head, say, "No way!" and replace it with a good thought. This will lead to fruit-full actions. Count on it!

Still Learning

There's always more to learn about growing God's fruit. Here are some other things to help you.

REFLECT GOD in everything you do $5.00

MIRRORS

Q How did God decide what was wrong and right?

A God is perfect and right. God's very nature is good, and whatever he does is right. Anything that is against God's nature is wrong. God's rules in the Bible tell us what he's like.

Remember that God tells us what is right and wrong because he loves us. His rules protect and guide us. It's like telling a baby not to touch a hot stove. We want to keep the baby safe. We make the rule because we love the baby. God tells us what to do for the same reason. He wants to take care of us, make us joyful, and help us live.

Q When I ask a question, why do you always tell me what the Bible says?

theory #1
Dad
output
INSERT
BIBLE

A The Bible is God's Word. When we read it, we learn what God is like and how he wants us to live. Think of the Bible as an instruction book, like the one for the family car. If we do what the book says, the car will run right. If something goes wrong, we can read the book and find out how to fix it. The Bible is God's instruction book for our lives. We need to read and study it so that we will run right and so God can fix things that go wrong with us. We also must do what the Bible says.

Q Is it OK to tell people to shut up if they're being jerks?

A When someone does something annoying or wrong, we don't have to like it. But we shouldn't do something bad in return. God wants us to be loving and kind. So the rule is to be respectful, not bossy or rude. If the person will listen, say something about it kindly. Sometimes it's *good* to tell friends that they're not being nice or they're being mean.

God knows that it's best for us when we do things his way. Responding to cruelty with kindness makes friends of people. But when we respond with cruelty, we just feed it and make more conflict. The best way to make someone stop annoying you is to be nice, not mean.

Q Why do some brothers and sisters fight?

A When you live with somebody, sometimes you get annoyed with each other, try to use the same thing, want the same space, or want to do things differently. This happens even in families where people love each other very much.

The next time you disagree with your brother or sister, state your differences without yelling or hitting. If you're upset, calm down and lower your voice. Tell the person how you feel. Try to see things from their point of view. Listen without interrupting. Then as you talk it out, suggest ways to solve the

problem. Remember, you're both on the same team.

Every conflict is an opportunity to learn one of life's most valuable skills—how to get along with others. It won't happen by magic. You have to learn how to do it, like learning to ride a bike. It takes work, prayer, and practice.

Adapted from *103 Questions Children Ask About Right from Wrong*, Tyndale House Publishers, 1995 and *106 Questions Children Ask About Our World*, Tyndale House Publishers, 1998. Used by permission.

Go For It!

Do you want to be all God created you to be? Do what God has planned for you to do? Make a difference in the lives of people around you? Be the best person, student, worker, child you can be? *Yes, yes,* **yes!** You're already on your way. You belong to God (you're his kid), and you're choosing his way. The guaranteed way to be all, do all, and have all God has for you is to let the Holy Spirit work inside you.

Change Is an Adventure!

By now, you should know beyond any doubt that God loves you and wants awesome things for you, even more than you can imagine! All you have to do is choose his way. Change can be tough, but God is the best teacher. He makes learning an adventure. He also puts people in our lives to help us, and for us to help: our parents, people at church, and wise Christian friends.

Remember though, *God* is producing the fruit in us. Our job? Pray every day for him to change and grow us. Tell him daily that we want only what he wants. And remember what we've learned. Forgetting it would be like digging the same hole over and over. We'd never get any building done!

When the toymaker polishes areas of our lives, like completed, painted toys, we use them. When we're developing the next "toy," we remember what we learned from the earlier ones, and we learn easier and faster.

It's all about God's love. He's with us, growing his fruit in us, changing us to be like his son. The results? Love, joy, peace, patience, kindness, goodness, faithfulness, gentleness, and self-control—in us, around us, and for us. What a life!